STEM Projects in **MINECRAFT**™

The Unofficial Guide to
Building Towns in
MINECRAFT™

ERIC J. TOWER

PowerKiDS
press

New York

Published in 2019 by The Rosen Publishing Group, Inc.
29 East 21st Street, New York, NY 10010

First Edition

Editor: Greg Roza
Book Design: Rachel Rising
Illustrator: Matías Lapegüe

Photo Credits: Cover, pp. 1, 3, 4, 6, 8, 10, 12, 14, 16, 18, 20, 22, 23, 24 (background) Evgeniy Dzyuba/Shutterstock.com; pp. 4, 8, 12, 14, 16, 18, 20 (insert) Levent Konuk/Shutterstock.com; p. 5 vm/E+/Getty Images; p. 17 Reza Estakhrian/Taxi/Getty Images; p. 22 Isarapic/Shutterstock.com.

Cataloging-in-Publication Data

Names: Tower, Eric J.
Title: The unofficial guide to building towns in Minecraft / Eric J. Tower.
Description: New York : PowerKids Press, 2019. | Series: STEM Projects in Minecraft | Includes glossary and index.
Identifiers: LCCN ISBN 9781538329498 (pbk.) | ISBN 9781538329474 (library bound) | ISBN 9781538329504 (6 pack)
Subjects: LCSH: Minecraft (Game)–Juvenile literature. | Minecraft (Video game)–Handbooks, manuals, etc.–Juvenile literature.
Classification: LCC GV1469.M55 T69 2019 | DDC 794.8–dc23

Manufactured in the United States of America

CPSIA Compliance Information: Batch #CS18PK: For Further Information contact Rosen Publishing, New York, New York at 1-800-237-9932

Contents

Let's Build a Town!

Have you ever wondered how the town you live in came to be? Who decided where the roads should go or where to put the buildings? It takes many different types of people working together over years to build a town. Civil engineers, city planners, **architects**, construction workers, and government officials all play important parts.

Minecraft is a sandbox game, which means players can move through the world, building and changing things. The world is made mostly of blocks of many **materials** we can use to build roads, houses, wells, farms, and anything else we'd like to have in our town. Let's get started!

MINECRAFT MANIA

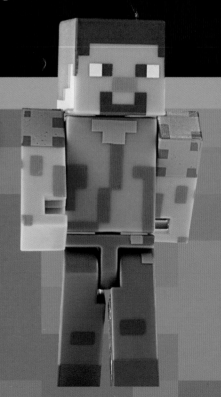

Minecraft can be played in several different **modes**. For **designing** and building a town, it's easiest to play in Creative mode. In this mode, you have an unlimited number of blocks that you would otherwise need to collect yourself.

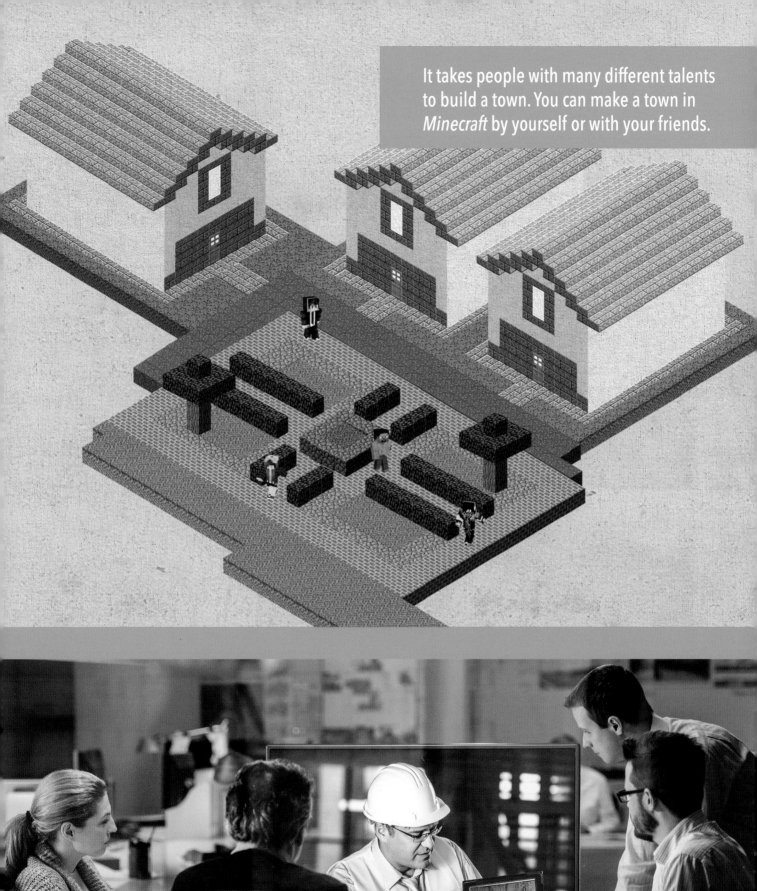

It takes people with many different talents to build a town. You can make a town in *Minecraft* by yourself or with your friends.

Finding a Place to Build

Civil engineers play an important part in the planning of a real-world town. These people decide what important **resources** the town needs, such as rivers or forests. They **survey** the land and then select a place to build. A civil engineer may also oversee the clearing of plants and leveling of the land for building.

In *Minecraft*, you can also play the part of a civil engineer. Select a plot of land that's 100 cubes by 100 cubes. A piece of land is called a parcel. You want to pick a parcel that is near three important resources: water, trees, and stone.

Preparing the Land

When you're building a *Minecraft* town, you'll also be the construction crew! No matter how difficult it is, it's your job to prepare the land for building based on the plans made by the civil engineer. You can start by chopping down all the trees in the parcel you selected for the town. Next, fill in any holes or pools of water with stone or dirt.

Real-world civil engineers must know if there are caves beneath their building site. It can be unsafe to build over caves! Just like in the real world, you may find a cave system under your *Minecraft* construction site.

MINECRAFT MANIA

If you find a cave system under your site in *Minecraft*, you might want to keep it so you can use its resources later. It won't **collapse**, unlike a real-world cave system.

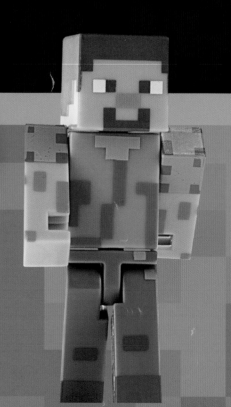

Real-world construction crews use large machines to clear and level the land. In *Minecraft* Creative mode, you can clear land simply by hitting the blocks that are in your way. In Survival mode, you can use tools such as shovels, pickaxes, and axes.

Designing the Town

In the real world, city planners look at the land to decide where to place roads and **utilities**. What parts of the town should have housing? Where should businesses go? How many police and fire stations are needed?

You can create your own town plan on a piece of graph paper. Start in the middle of your parcel and draw roads into the nearest forest, down to the nearest water source, and out to the nearest source of stone. Next, draw a wall around the outside of your parcel. Finally, shade in areas of town where you want farms, livestock pens, houses, and other buildings.

When planning your wall, remember to leave space to build a gate and guardhouse at each road. Don't forget to use strong stone. There are lots of monsters out there!

Critical Infrastructure

Critical infrastructure includes the buildings and utilities that are important to a town and the people in it. In the real world, this infrastructure includes pipes that bring water, wires that bring electricity, roads that bring people to town, and even farms that provide food.

In *Minecraft*, critical infrastructure includes farms, water sources, roads, and a mine within easy reach of town. Farms are the most important of these things. Place them where they will get the most sunlight and won't be in the shadow of tall buildings. *Minecraft* plants, like real plants, need a certain amount of light to grow.

MINECRAFT MANIA

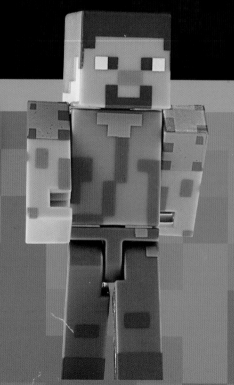

Redstone provides power very similar to electricity in *Minecraft*. Tunnels and spaces under your town can allow you to wire the buildings for power.

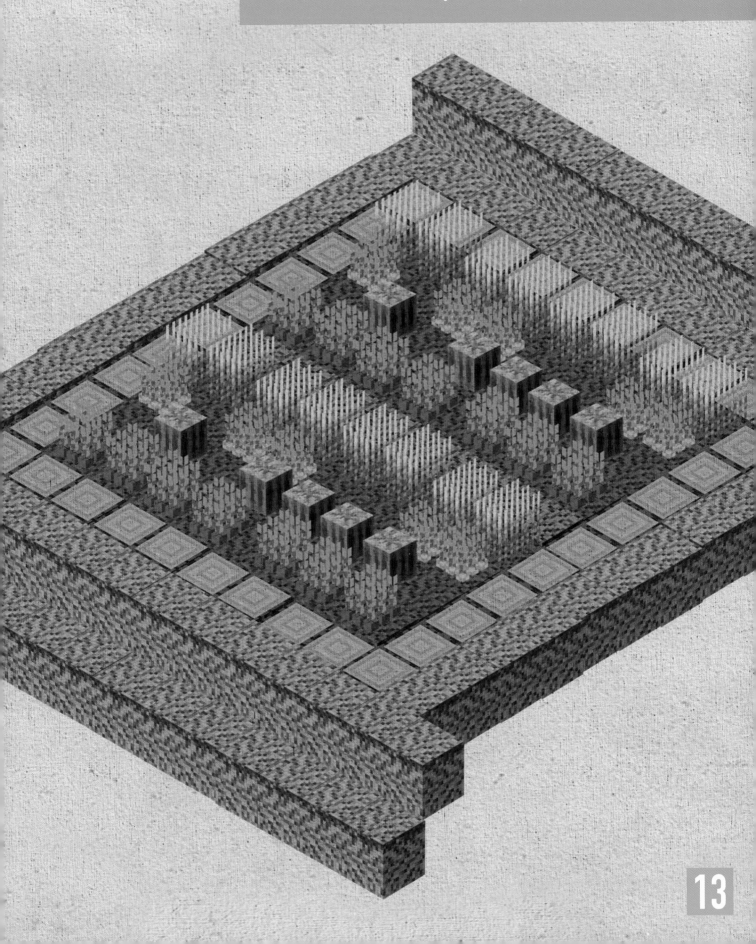

Water can **hydrate** dirt for farming up to four blocks in every direction. There are many different plans you can use for farms.

Protecting the Town

Historically, people built walls around cities to protect them from enemies and wild animals. Today, government officials also create public safety plans to protect their people from a wide number of threats, including fires and natural disasters.

In *Minecraft*, you need to protect your town from fire too. Building with stone will help you do this. You also need to protect your town from many types of monster threats, including zombies, skeletons, creepers, and giant spiders! Walls will help keep monsters from getting into your town. Be sure spiders can't climb over the wall by putting an overhang on it.

MINECRAFT MANIA

Lighting is important protection for a *Minecraft* town. Monsters appear anywhere that isn't well lit. You'll want to have light sources, such as torches, throughout the town to stop monsters from appearing.

Having a guardhouse with a fence gate on both ends allows you to bring livestock in and out of town without having to open the town to monsters. If a monster gets past the first fence gate, it will be trapped in the guardhouse.

Building Foundations

As civil engineers and city planners work on critical infrastructure, architects design **blueprints** for buildings. The first thing each building needs is a **foundation**. In the real world, foundations are very important. They **distribute** the weight of the building so the building doesn't sink into the soil. The larger the building, the larger and deeper the foundation must be.

In *Minecraft*, you don't have to worry about this. Still, foundations are helpful for planning how a town will look before you put up the rest of the buildings. And you can hide cool things such as redstone **mechanisms** and treasure chests in them!

MINECRAFT MANIA

Workers have to dig deep to build the foundation for something as tall as a skyscraper. This isn't necessary in *Minecraft*, because gravity doesn't work as it does in the real world.

The first step when building a foundation in the real world is to dig into the earth. You don't have to do that in *Minecraft*, but you can! This space can serve as a basement or even a secret hideaway.

Building Housing

City planners and architects work together to make sure there's enough housing for everyone expected to live in a town. There also needs to be room so the town can grow over time. It's important to make sure you have resources available to build these houses and support the people.

In *Minecraft*, the number of villagers in your town will grow based on the number of houses with doors. You can use a mix of wood and stone to build houses. Stone is tough and one of the easiest resources to find, but wood from trees is a renewable resource. Keep planting new trees!

MINECRAFT MANIA

Creating the proper balance between houses and villagers will take some experiments. You can find tutorials on how to fine-tune the growth of villagers online.

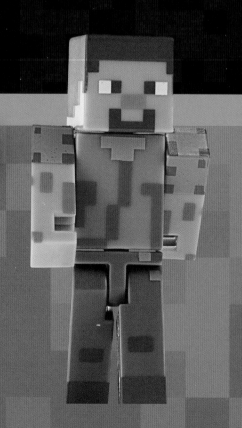

These house blueprints will help you grow your villager population. Don't stop with just one house. Fill in the whole neighborhood—more houses, more villagers!

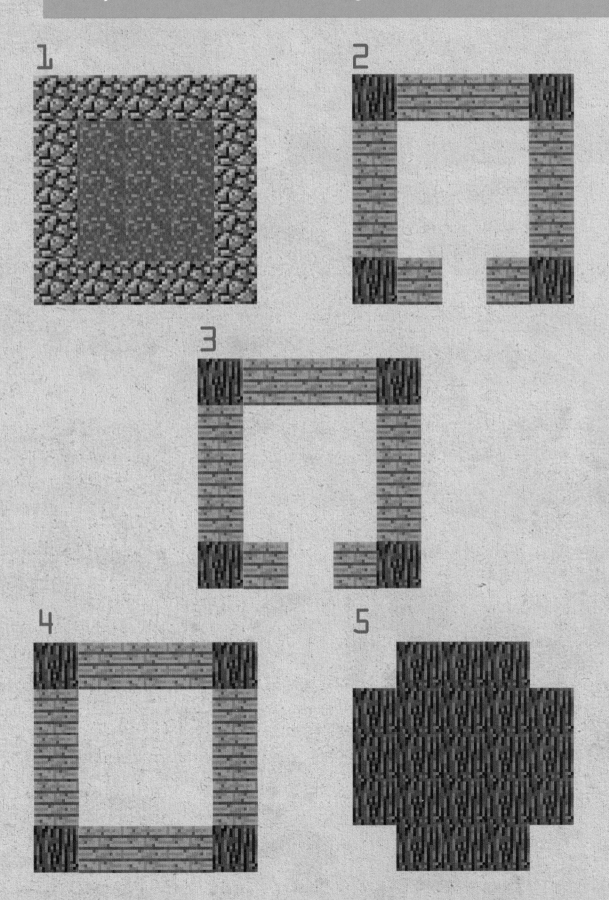

Creating Industry

In the real world, planners often try to keep businesses and factories near other businesses and factories. This helps keep pollution and traffic away from neighborhoods where people live. In *Minecraft*, you might also want to separate houses from other buildings. This could prevent the spread of fire from blacksmith shops or the escape of livestock from holding pens.

Minecraft towns often have blacksmiths, libraries, butcher shops, and sometimes churches. What types of businesses will you create for your town? Using basic blueprints for a house, how many other types of buildings can you make? What if you make them two levels tall?

MINECRAFT MANIA

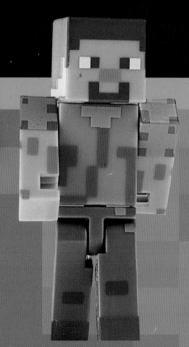

Now that you understand the basics of how to plan and build a town, look into all the different types of materials *Minecraft* allows you to use. You can pave the streets with gold!

Experiment with the layout of your town. If you don't like it, knock it down and build it again. Towns can take on interesting shapes as old buildings and new constructions blend together.

21

Making Mods

You can make your *Minecraft* creations even more exciting with modifications, or mods. Using a computer program called ScriptCraft, you can create new blocks, change the way the game functions, and make your own games. Imagine what you could build! You could make a house that looks just like your real-world home or create a town that's hidden underwater!

If you're interested in learning how to create mods in *Minecraft*, visit the website below. You'll find the information needed to get started with ScriptCraft and build your own *Minecraft* mods.

https://scriptcraftjs.org

Glossary

architect: A person who designs buildings.

blueprint: A plan for how a building will be made.

collapse: To fall down suddenly and completely.

design: To create the pattern or shape of something. Also, the pattern or shape of something.

distribute: Sharing or spreading something out.

foundation: A prepared base or support.

hydrate: To add water to something.

material: Something from which something else can be made.

mechanism: A piece of machinery.

mode: A form of something that is different from other forms of the same thing.

resource: Something that can be used.

survey: To measure and examine an area of land.

utility: A business organization that provides a public service for homes and businesses, such as electricity, heat, etc.

Index

Websites

Due to the changing nature of Internet links, PowerKids Press has developed an online list of websites related to the subject of this book. This site is updated regularly. Please use this link to access the list:
www.powerkidslinks.com/stemmc/towns

Biomass Power

Richard and Louise Spilsbury

PowerKiDS
press™
New York

Published in 2012 by
The Rosen Publishing Group Inc.
29 East 21st Street,
New York, NY 10010

First Edition

Editorial Director: Rasha Elsaeed
Produced for Wayland by Discovery Books Ltd
Managing Editor: Rachel Tisdale
Designer: Ian Winton
Illustrator: Stefan Chabluk
Picture Researcher: Tom Humphrey

Library of Congress Cataloging-in-Publication Data

Spilsbury, Richard, 1963-
Biomass power / by Richard Spilsbury and Louise Spilsbury. – 1st ed.
    p. cm. – (Let's discuss energy resources)
Includes index.
ISBN 978-1-4488-5260-4 (lib. bdg.)
1. Biomass energy–Juvenile literature. I. Spilsbury, Louise. II. Title. III. Series.

TP339.S657 2012
333.95'39–dc22

2010046941

Photographs:
Choren: title page & p. 9; Corbis: p. 18 (Everett Kennedy Brown/epa), p. 22 (David Sailors), p. 29 (Szilard Koszticsak/epa); Getty Images: p. 25 (Kambou Sia/AFP), p. 28 (Ben Stansall/AFP); Honda: p. 5; Istockphoto.com: p. 21; Newscast: cover main (E.ON UK), p. 11 (E.ON UK); Photographers Direct: p. 4 (Paul Glendell/www.glendell.co.uk); Sandia National Laboratories: p. 24 (Randy Wong); Shutterstock: cover background (Hywit Dimyadi), p. 6 (Lucian Coman), p. 7 & imprint page (Inacio Pires), p. 15, p. 27 (Dr Morley Read); USDA: p. 13 (Keith Weller); U.S. Navy: p. 20 (Chief Mass Communications Specialist Philip A Fortman); Wikimedia: p. 12 (Dirk Ingo Franke), p. 14 (Steven Vaughan), p. 16 (Klaus Schenck).

Manufactured in China
CPSIA Compliance Information: Batch #WAS1102PK: For Further Information
contact Rosen Publishing, New York, New York at 1-800-237-9932

Contents

The words in **bold** can be found in the glossary on page 31.

Biomass as an Energy Resource

We use many different energy resources to help us do work, such as sunlight to warm greenhouses so plants grow quicker. Fuels are concentrated stores of energy. We generally release energy by burning them. Coal and oil are **fossil fuels**, formed underground millions of years ago. Wood, however, is an example of biomass—fuel harvested or processed from living things.

Wood chips are one type of biomass. This fuel is burned like coal in a boiler to release energy for heating water.

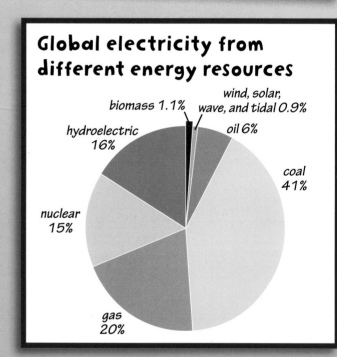

Global electricity from different energy resources

biomass 1.1%
wind, solar, wave, and tidal 0.9%
hydroelectric 16%
oil 6%
coal 41%
nuclear 15%
gas 20%

Global Electricity

Energy from burning fuel is also used to generate electricity in power plants. Most electricity is generated using fossil fuels. The next most important energy resource is **hydroelectric power**, which uses the force of moving water. At present, biomass only produces just over 1 percent of the world's electricity.

Impacts of Using Fossil Fuels

Burning fossil fuels in power stations and also in engines that move vehicles releases large amounts of gases such as carbon dioxide. Carbon dioxide traps heat in the atmosphere, gradually raising the average temperature on Earth. The impacts of this **global warming** include extreme weather that can harm living things and spoil crops. Other gases from fossil fuels cause air pollution. Extracting fossil fuels from under the ground also damages the environment.

Types of Energy Resources

As well as contributing to global warming, fossil fuels are a **nonrenewable** energy resource. World supplies of fossil fuels are finite. Once we have used them up, there will be no more, and they are running out. Also, fossil fuels are only found in certain places on Earth, so some countries may not have easy access to these resources. We need to find other sources of energy to replace fossil fuels.

Energy resources that will not run out in the future are **renewable**. Biomass is renewable since more can be planted or harvested once it is burned. Other renewable energy resources include hydroelectric, solar power (energy from sunlight), wind power from moving air, wave and tidal power from moving seawater, and geothermal power, which is energy from hot rocks underground.

Nearly every car on the road runs on fossil fuel. Each year, over 50 million new cars are produced.

Why discuss biomass power?

Biomass can be grown or produced all over the world. Unlike the other renewables, biomass can be burned and used in many of the power stations and vehicles that use fossil fuels at the moment. However, while using renewables generally does not release harmful gases, burning biomass does. This book looks at the range of biomass options available and discusses their advantages and disadvantages compared to other energy resources now and into the future.

What Is Biomass?

Biomass fuel includes solids, liquids, and gases ranging from wood to alcohol made from corn crops. All biomass is **organic** and comes from living or recently living organisms, mostly plants. Since all plants need sunlight to grow, biomass energy comes primarily from the Sun.

Type of Biomass

The commonest type of biomass used globally is wood from trees or other woody plants. Wood was the major global fuel before the eighteenth century, when fossil fuels were first widely used by people. **Fuelwood** remains the only available cooking fuel for billions of people in many less developed parts of the world. Another type of biomass is waste, such as crop, industrial, and household waste and animal manure.

Biomass may be burned directly or processed in different ways to make fuels for burning. Biomass can be processed into charcoal, which is made by carefully heating pieces of wood. It can also be processed into liquid **biofuels**, such as alcohol and oils. Biofuels are often made from crops such as corn and oil palm, and these fuels have several advantages over charcoal. They yield a higher percentage of energy than unprocessed biomass.

In some African countries, fuelwood supplies over 90 percent of energy. Some African people harvest their own, as here, but many others spend large amounts of their low earnings on fuelwood.

Trapping the Sun's Energy

All biomass starts off as green plants. Green plants make their food using **photosynthesis**. They use solar energy to convert carbon dioxide and water into stored, chemical energy in the form of sugars. Plants use these sugars to live and grow. Fossil fuels are ancient biomass that has been changed by the high temperatures and pressures underground.

Green plants hold their leaves up toward the Sun to capture energy for conversion via photosynthesis into biomass.

Let's Discuss

Biomass vs. fossil fuels.

Advantages:

Renewable
Once biomass is harvested, more can be replanted on the same land. Waste is also an enormous resource, and more is constantly being made.

Grows Anywhere
Biomass may be grown all around the world, whereas fossil fuels are only found in certain places, and often deep underground.

Disadvantages:

Less Concentrated
Burning wood that is not completely dry releases about half the energy per ton that coal does.

Processed Fuels
It takes more energy to process biofuels than to extract the equivalent weight of fossil fuels.

On balance, biomass is probably better than coal in that it is available everywhere and it is renewable.

From Wood to Fuel

Biomass fuel for use in power stations and in boilers heating water or air inside buildings can be harvested from trees in natural forests, but it is usually taken from **plantations**. These are managed areas of land planted with woody or other tough crops. Waste wood from the timber industry can also be used as biomass. Most biomass is then dried, cut, or processed in different ways so that it burns efficiently.

Plantation Crops

Biomass plantation crops need to be fast-growing to ensure that new crops are available just months or years after the old ones have been cut down. The plants should also make thick tissue with a high carbon content that releases lots of energy when it burns. The plantation crops grown worldwide depend on the **climate** of a region. Willow and poplar grow in colder climates, while eucalyptus thrives in warmer climates. Sugar cane, elephant grass, and switchgrass are grown on many biomass plantations. Vast forest plantations in areas such as Canada, Russia, and Finland are mostly grown for timber for use in the building or paper industry. The unwanted parts of trees, from bark to sawdust, are also important sources of biomass.

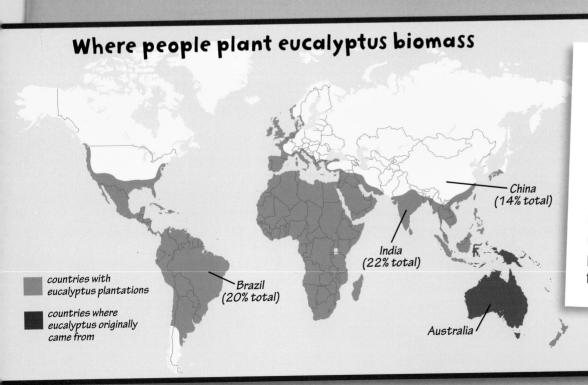

Where people plant eucalyptus biomass

China (14% total)

India (22% total)

Brazil (20% total)

Australia

countries with eucalyptus plantations

countries where eucalyptus originally came from

Eucalyptus grows naturally in Australia. It is now grown on plantations in warm places worldwide as fast-growing biomass. Over half of the total world eucalyptus crop is produced in just three countries.

Making Fuel

Biomass burns best when it is dry, so wood is often left to dry naturally in huge sheds. It can also be dried using heating machines, although this is more expensive because the process requires electricity. Smaller pieces of biomass burn more easily and efficiently than large pieces. Therefore, larger pieces of wood are often cut into small pieces, called chips, before use. Sawdust, grass, and other less dense biomass, however, is pressed into pellets or large blocks that burn more gradually than sawdust would.

A special harvesting machine cuts and chips a row of willow saplings in Sweden.

CASE STUDY — Willow Plantations in Sweden

Willow trees were first planted as biomass for heating in Sweden in the 1970s. This was when supplies of oil from the Middle East were interrupted and oil became expensive. Today, willow biomass is also used in many Swedish power plants. Willow grows easily from cuttings taken from other willow trees and it thrives in the cold temperatures and soil types found in Sweden. Willow trees are **coppiced** 3–5 years after planting. This means they are cut down to near ground level, the biomass is removed, and the trees then regrow. Willow trees can be coppiced five to ten times through their 25–30-year life span.

How Biomass Power Plants Work

A biomass power plant works like a fossil fuel power plant. It converts chemical energy in fuel into heat energy, then movement or kinetic energy, and finally into electrical energy.

From Fuel to Electricity

Conveyor belts carry biomass fuel into a very hot oven called a furnace. The burning fuel heats water running through pipes in the furnace. The water turns into steam that is blasted against the blades of a turbine. The turbine blades spin under the force of the steam and this turns a machine called a generator. This rotates magnets that causes electricity to flow from coiled wires.

Some fossil fuel power stations burn a mix of coal and biomass to reduce the amount of **greenhouse gas** created. This is called **cofiring**. Often, the biomass is turned into gas first, in a process called gasification, which also removes impurities that would create soot when burned. The gas burns better than solid biomass.

Reusing Heat

In some power stations, steam-filled pipes pass through heat exchangers to cool the steam back into water. Water in the heat exchanger absorbs the heat, and the resulting hot water may be piped to homes for heating and washing. This reuse of heat is called **combined heat and power**.

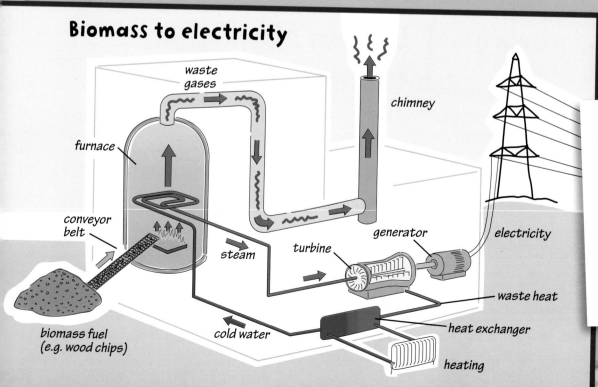

Biomass to electricity

waste gases

chimney

furnace

conveyor belt

steam

turbine

generator

electricity

biomass fuel (e.g. wood chips)

cold water

waste heat

heat exchanger

heating

This diagram shows how heat energy from burning biomass is used to generate electricity and then for heating in a combined heat and power system.

Energy and Power

Energy is the ability to do work, measured in joules. Power is the rate at which energy is used or sent, measured in joules per second, or watts. For example, a dryer needs around 4,000 joules each second to dry clothes. A typical combined heat and power biomass power plant can generate a maximum of 5–10 million watts (or megawatts—MW). Enormous power stations such as Drax, UK, which cofire biomass with coal, can generate nearly four hundred times as much as a biomass power station. However, no power station keeps running all the time. We compare use or output over time using kWh—thousand watts per hour.

Logs stockpiled for use as fuel outside Steven's Croft biomass power station, Lockerbie, Scotland.

CASE STUDY

Mixed Fuel Power in India

The biomass power plant at Chilakapalem, Andhra Pradesh, India, burns a range of leftover waste from local agricultural industries. These include rice husks, peanut shells, crushed sugar cane stalks, and waste from local mills. The fuel is very cheap to buy and there is plenty of it, but the electricity output of the power station varies through the year because it often has to be shut down while ash left after burning the biomass is cleaned out. An average person in India uses just under 500 kWh each year. In general, it takes about 2.2 lb. (1 kg) of biomass to generate each kWh at the Chilakapalem power plant.

Energy from Waste

Organic waste produced by individuals, communities, farms, and industries is an energy resource that can be used as biomass for heating and also for electricity generation.

Found Fuel

In isolated parts of China and Africa, where there is little available fuelwood, waste animal dung is often collected, dried, and burned for cooking or heating. Barbecues that burn pellets made from waste such as straw are increasingly popular for cooking in many less developed countries such as India. Since they contain more energy per pound, waste pellets are more energy efficient than fuelwood, so families can spend less time searching for fuelwood each day.

Landfill Gas

Landfill gas is a fuel that seeps from waste dumps. Organic waste, such as waste food, garden cuttings, and cardboard, rots or **decomposes**. During this process, **bacteria** feed on the waste, producing some heat but also methane gas and carbon dioxide. In some sites, landfill gas is collected as a fuel. It is processed to remove carbon dioxide and water that would prevent it burning efficiently, and then used in furnaces to heat water for local buildings or to create steam for electricity generation. In some rural parts of China and Nepal, communities put animal and human manure and food remains into **biodigesters**. These produce gas in a similar way to landfill sites, which is used for lighting and heating.

Some biomass power stations, such as this facility in Germany, use methane gas from decomposed farm animal manure as fuel.

Waste Direct to Electricity

Many types of waste are burned directly in power stations. These include crop waste such as sugar cane stems, industrial waste, and landfill waste. In Malmö, Sweden, around half a million tons of landfill waste is burned each year to supply 40 percent of the city's hot water and generate 10 percent of its electricity.

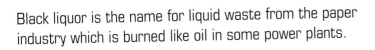

Black liquor is the name for liquid waste from the paper industry which is burned like oil in some power plants.

Let's Discuss

Waste is a good source of biomass.

Yes:

Clears Waste Mountains
Of the 2 billion tons of waste dumped each year, only around one-third is recycled. Using waste for energy means fewer landfill sites.

Free Fuel
Waste is free, and in some cases, cities and countries pay power companies to take it away, so the electricity produced should be inexpensive.

No:

Dangerous Smoke
Burning waste such as plastic produces smoke that contains harmful chemicals such as dioxins. These can cause cancers when breathed in.

Preventing Recycling
Giving waste a value as an energy resource may mean people recycle less. Then companies will need to use more raw materials such as oil to make new things.

On balance, the benefits of clearing waste mountains and making cheap power outweigh the dangers of burning waste.

Biofuels

Biofuels are liquid fuels that can be used to power cars and other vehicles. They are mostly made from energy crops—biomass grown especially for use as fuel.

Producing Biofuel

Bioethanol, or **fuel ethanol,** is produced worldwide from plant parts that are rich in sugar. Around 90 percent of all bioethanol is produced in Brazil, from sugar cane, and in the United States, from corn. Sugar cane is pressed to extract sugary syrup. Corn is soaked in hot water and ground up to release the starch, which is then converted into sugar using acid. Yeast is added to the sugar and substances called **enzymes** in the yeast convert the sugar into bioethanol and also carbon dioxide. Bioethanol is generally mixed with gasoline before being used as fuel. For example, in Brazil, all gasoline contains 25 percent ethanol, while in the U.S., most cars can run on a 10 percent blend.

At this biofuel factory, biomass is stored in the large tanks on the right and the sugars it contains are turned into bioethanol in the part of the factory with the chimney.

Using alcohol to run cars is not a new idea. Car pioneers of the early twentieth century, including Henry Ford, designed engines that ran on alcohol, but when oil became cheaper, all car manufacturers started to use that fuel.

Plant Diesel

Most **biodiesel** is made from oils pressed from sunflower seeds, oil palm seeds, soybeans, rapeseed, and sunflower seeds. Some biodiesel is made from filtered waste oils and animal fats, from sources such as restaurants and factories. Some diesel vehicles, such as cargo ships, can burn the oils as they are. Most vehicles use oils that have been processed with alcohol, because then they burn more easily. Biodiesel is used more than bioethanol in Europe, yet even in a country that uses large volumes, such as Germany, it only accounts for less than 5 percent of total diesel use. Increasing amounts of oils for biodiesel are exported from Asia, South America, and Africa for use in Europe and North America because they are cheap and plentiful to buy.

A pile of oil palm bunches waiting for processing. The bunches are shaken to remove fruit, which are then mashed and pressed to remove the oil inside.

CASE STUDY — Clean Streets in Austria

The government of the Austrian city of Graz used to collect cooking oil from households and restaurants because when oil was poured down sinks, it clogged the city's drains. Today, the government collect oil for processing into biodiesel because Graz is committed to using less normal diesel in its bid to reduce the air pollution in the city. All public buses in Graz now run on biodiesel, and the city's largest private taxi company aims to run over half of its fleet on this fuel by 2020.

Land Impacts of Biomass Power

Demand for biomass—and in particular, biofuels—is rising. Globally, there is a shortage of farmland, so space to grow biomass is created by clearing rain forests and other **habitats**. Land that is reused to harvest more biomass is often farmed intensively—using heavy machines and chemicals to speed up the growth of the plants.

Clearing Forests

Cutting down forests, or **deforestation**, for biomass plantations is contributing significantly to the loss of rain forest in tropical countries. The major biomass crops that are threatening rain forests are soybeans in South America and oil palm through Southeast Asia and Africa. When forest is cut down, there is less space for animals, especially large ones such as tigers that travel long distances to find food. The plantations that replace the wild forests have only one type of plant growing in them, and the people that manage them interfere with the environment. That is why plantations generally contain few different types of animals, or have a lower **biodiversity**, than natural forests.

> *"If we run our cars on biofuels produced in the tropics... we are effectively burning rain forests in our gas tanks."*
>
> Dr. Holly Gibbs, Stanford University, California, 2009

Companies deforested land to plant this oil palm plantation in Ecuador. The plantation has lower biodiversity than the rain forest in the background, partly because workers spray chemicals to stop other plants growing there.

Environmental Effects

Deforestation is often concentrated in places where forest grows on **peat** soil that is naturally rich in **nutrients**. Biomass crops grow well on the cleared land. However, many tropical soils are low in nutrients, so plantation owners often apply large amounts of fertilizer to the soil in order to grow their crops quickly on deforested land. They use heavy machinery to farm the land and this can damage the soil, which means it holds even fewer nutrients. Damaged soils can dry out and can be blown or washed away easily into rivers and lakes. There the chemical fertilizers affect aquatic animals and plants and harm these habitats.

Let's Discuss

Is biofuel production the major cause of deforestation?

Yes:

Rain Forest Lost
Massive areas of rain forest have been cut down to make room for biomass plantations. When Indonesia's palm oil production grew from the 1990s onward, it lost an area of forest twice the size of Louisiana.

Growing Problem
Biofuels command high prices on world markets, so some countries are allowing more deforestation by not protecting areas of rain forest.

No:

Other Culprits
Logging and mining are the major causes of deforestation. The food and cosmetics industries also use large amounts of palm oil.

Improving the Situation
In some places, plantation owners protect areas of rain forest within their cropland and farm in ways that do not damage the growing environment.

On balance, logging companies are still the major cause of deforestation, but biomass plantations are a growing cause for concern.

Atmospheric Impacts of Biomass

Growing biomass removes carbon dioxide from the atmosphere, but its production and use release gases that have negative impacts on the world's atmosphere, including global warming and air pollution.

Carbon Neutral

Biomass is often described as a carbon neutral fuel. This is because the amount of carbon dioxide released into the atmosphere by burning biomass is balanced by the amount removed from the atmosphere by photosynthesis as the biomass grows. Fossil fuels, on the other hand, have a negative effect on atmospheric carbon dioxide. They are the remains of biomass that photosynthesized millions of years ago, so they cannot absorb carbon dioxide to balance the gases released when they burn.

Global Warming

However, using biomass does produce greenhouse gases. Factories that make fertilizers to grow biomass or that process biofuels burn fossil fuels or use electricity to work. Most electricity is generated in fossil fuel power plants. Scientists estimate that clearing 2.5 acres (1 hectare) of rain forest by burning the trees releases 280 cubic tons (200 cubic tonnes) of carbon dioxide into the atmosphere. Decomposition of cleared soils, especially peat soils, also releases methane, another greenhouse gas.

Trucks are tipped up on ramps to quickly empty their biomass load at power plants. Road transportation releases 2.2 lb. (1 kg) of carbon dioxide for every 10 tons carried 0.6 mile (1 km).

Air Pollution

Burning biomass releases other polluting gases, such as carbon monoxide and nitrous and sulfur oxides, as well as soot or smoke particles into the atmosphere. All of these can affect the health of people who breathe them in. People who burn lots of fuelwood indoors, mostly in less developed parts of the world, can develop eye problems, breathing difficulties, throat cancer, and kidney problems as a result of breathing in smoke. It is estimated that 1.6 million people die each year as a result of sickness brought about by inhaling wood smoke.

Let's Discuss

Biomass is better for the atmosphere than fossil fuels.

Yes:

Less Carbon Dioxide
Burning biomass can release more carbon dioxide per ton than coal or gas, but this almost balances the amount it removes from the atmosphere during growth. The plants making fossil fuels died millions of years ago.

Cleaner Atmosphere
Burning biodiesel releases half the amount of air pollution than burning diesel produced from fossil fuels.

No:

Bad Biomass
The processing of some type of biomass, such as corn, into bioethanol requires more energy than this fuel releases when it is burned.

Other Greenhouse Gases
Methane and nitrous oxides released when using plantation fertilizers trap more heat than carbon dioxide.

Biomass is generally better for the atmosphere than fossil fuels because growing plants absorb atmospheric carbon dioxide.

How Biomass Power Affects People

The biggest impact on people from biomass power, apart from global warming, is the use of farmland to grow crops for energy rather than for food, and using food crops themselves as biomass. This affects the cost and availability of food and can cause social changes in communities, too.

Food or Fuel?

Biomass is in demand and can be sold for high prices. Many farmers have decided to grow and sell biofuel crops such as corn, sugar cane, and other crops instead of food crops. This has caused the price of foodstuffs such as wheat and rice to increase because there is less supply. At the same time, the amount of **food aid** given to very poor countries is decreasing because countries such as the United States, which need lots of biofuel, have less surplus corn to give away. This is causing a food crisis in many less developed countries. In 2008, The World Bank, a global financial institution, estimated that 75 percent of the worldwide price rise in food was caused by biofuel production.

Ethiopia is one country where so much farmland is used to grow biomass that many people need food aid from other countries to survive.

"It takes the same amount of grain to fill an SUV [people carrier] with ethanol as it does to feed a person."
Barbara Stocking, Oxfam, 2008

Impacts

In some places, people are being forced off their land to make way for biomass plantations. In 2007, the Colombian army bombed and invaded villages in the Choco region of Colombia because they claimed the villagers were hiding terrorists. People fled the region and then palm oil companies moved into the area to create plantations for biodiesel. Villagers who tried to move back were forced to sell their land cheaply to plantation owners.

However, biomass can have positive social and economic impacts, too. Its production provides jobs for farmers, transporters, and processors, and so brings wealth to some communities. Sixty percent of Brazilian bioethanol is produced in the São Paulo region of Brazil. The increased wealth this has brought has improved life for many by financing more schools and hospitals.

CASE STUDY — Hungarian Wetlands

The riverbanks of the Tisza wetlands, Hungary, are being gradually taken over by a weed called indigobush. A project involving the charity WWF and AES Hungary, a local power company, is clearing and coppicing the indigobush for biomass. This seasonal work is providing jobs for underprivileged Roma people, who live for part of the year in the region. It also keeps the wetland waters clear for waterbirds, fish, and other wildlife.

The WWF biomass project is one way to help the Tisza wetlands in Hungary remain an unspoiled habitat.

The Cost of Biomass Power

The success or failure of biomass power as an energy resource is largely dependent on its costs relative to other power sources. The cost of electricity or biofuel to consumers is generally the total of the cost of growing or getting the fuel and the cost of running power plants or fuel-processing factories.

Setting Up Biomass

Setting up biomass power begins with buying or clearing land, including the cost of machinery and workers. Growing plants for biodiesel in particular needs lots of land, because the yield of the oil per plant is low. Scientists have calculated that a year's harvest from crops covering 30 football fields could only supply fuel for a one-way transatlantic flight! Then there is the cost of the seeds or plants, water, and fertilizers to help grow the crop, and the harvesting and processing costs. For biomass electricity, costs can also include adapting fossil fuel power stations for cofiring, or building a new power station. Steven's Croft in Scotland, is the UK's biggest biomass power station—it generates up to 44 MW of electricity at any one time and cost $135 million to build. Costs can only be recouped once the biofuel or biomass electricity is being bought by consumers.

The cost of constructing a new bioethanol factory, such as this one in Indianapolis, Indiana, is around $150 million.

Comparing Costs

It is tricky to compare the costs of biomass with other kinds of power for various reasons. For example, bioethanol from Brazil is cheaper than that from the United States, because labor and processing costs are much lower in Brazil. The cost of producing biomass electricity also varies depending on the fuel used. Using landfill gas is as cheap as using coal or hydroelectric power, but using gasified wood chip costs around twice as much as using natural gas, because of the processing costs.

Let's Discuss

Biomass is a cheap source of power.

Yes:

Local Fuel
Biomass electricity is generally cheapest when fuel is sourced from places near to power plants, because there are lower transportation costs.

No Expensive Technology
Wind, solar, and wave power need expensive machines to harness energy, but biomass is burned in existing power stations and vehicles.

No:

Cost of Global Warming
Using biomass can add to global warming. A 2006 UK government review estimated the cost of dealing with global warming at $7.5 trillion.

Environmental Costs
The loss of animals and plants owing to deforestation for biomass plantations is both important and potentially costly. For example, plants that could be used to make life-saving medicines may become extinct.

Biomass is a cheap source of power, but its production contributes to the costs of global warming and environmental destruction.

23

How Governments Help Biomass

Around the world, countries have resolved to use fewer fossil fuels in order to slow global warming. Different governments are reducing carbon dioxide emissions by encouraging power companies to produce, and their public to buy, more biofuel and biomass-power electricity.

Agreements

In the early 1990s, members of the United Nations (UN) formally agreed that there was a link between fossil fuel use and increased global warming. At meetings since then in venues such as Kyoto, Japan, and Copenhagen, Denmark, many countries have made agreements to cut carbon dioxide emissions by different amounts. One way governments can meet targets is by making power companies switch some electricity generation from fossil fuels to renewables. For instance, from 2005 onward, the Chinese government pledged to supply 15 percent of all its country's energy needs from renewable sources. The UK's Didcot power station cofires some sawdust with coal to help meet the country's targets.

Power companies that are struggling to meet agreed targets, while generating what their customers use, may buy carbon credits. These are payments for emission reductions from burning renewable fuels in other countries. For example, a landfill gas power station in Kunming, China, prevents 70,000 tons (64,000 tonnes) of methane reaching the atmosphere each year by using it as fuel. Carbon credits for that emission reduction were bought by an Italian power company to meet its targets.

U.S. government laboratories and car makers such as General Motors are encouraging scientists at fuel companies to develop economic ways of making cheap biofuel in future.

A Helping Hand

Governments often subsidize, or pay to encourage increased biomass and biofuel production. They usually raise the money from taxes, money paid to governments by their citizens. From 1996 to 2008, the U.S. government paid around $56 billion in subsidies to bioethanol producers to make sure that millions more gallons of this biofuel was used in the U.S. by 2012. This has resulted in many U.S. farmers switching to growing corn just for biomass, which has contributed to the increase in global food prices. Since 2008, the U.S. government has started to subsidize more of the technologies that make biomass power from crop waste and other sources, rather than corn.

CASE STUDY — Jatropha in Ghana

Jatropha is a weedlike crop that produces many oil-rich seeds that are ideal for biodiesel production. In 2009, the government of Ghana sold hundreds of thousands of acres of farmland to around 20 oil companies from countries including Israel, Germany, Norway, and India. These companies hope to grow jatropha cheaply and sell the biodiesel at a profit around the world. Burning biodiesel releases less carbon dioxide than burning normal diesel, so investing in jatropha will help the companies meet the targets for emission cuts from their products requested by their governments. The Ghanaian government makes money, but the country loses farmland for food crops and also scarce water because the foreign companies take it to irrigate their crops.

Jatropha can grow on wasteland in dry places, but produces a much bigger crop of seeds when grown on irrigated farmland.

New Biomass Technology

Scientists worldwide are looking for new raw materials and new techniques to produce more and better biomass for burning and for biofuels. Many solutions are adaptations of existing ones, such as developing better strains of corn that need less fertilizer, and hence less energy, to grow. These are a few of the newer ideas.

Growing Algae for Oil

Algae, or water weeds, are a promising new source of biodiesel because around half of their weight may consist of oil. The algae are grown in sunlight in open ponds or clear plastic bags and fed with nutrients. They can also be grown in dark tanks with sugar as food. The algae are usually harvested and pressed to release the oil, but some scientists are investigating a way of adding chemicals that effectively "milk" the oil from the algae without killing them. Scientists believe that eventually algae might be able to yield over 23,775 gallons (90,000 liters) of biodiesel per 2.5 acres (1 hectare) at a cost of $1.60 a gallon ($0.40 a liter). However, at present, the process is experimental so small amounts of oil are being extracted at a high cost. The biodiesel from this oil is currently much too expensive—over $32 per gallon ($8 per liter)—for any vehicle to use.

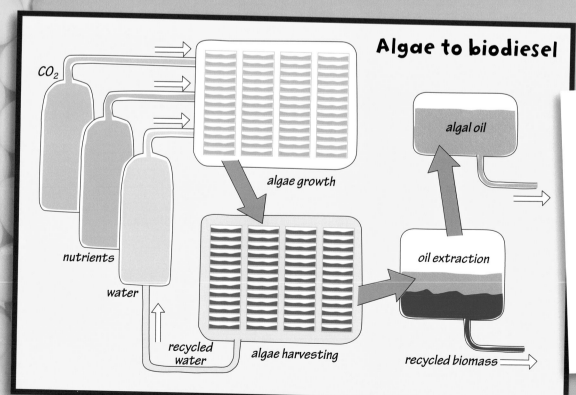

Algae to biodiesel

CO₂

nutrients

water

algae growth

recycled water

algae harvesting

oil extraction

recycled biomass

algal oil

The algae are provided with water, carbon dioxide, and nutrients to photosynthesize and grow fast. After harvest by filtering out the algae, the remaining water is reused for more algae to live in.

Processing Waste

Many types of biomass waste, such as straw, waste wood, and even the fibrous remains of pressed sugar cane, are mostly made of tough cellulose. They contain only small amounts of the sugar or starch needed to make them into biofuel. Scientists are looking at ways of adding enzymes to break down the cellulose into sugars that can then be processed into bioethanol.

Scientists studied bacteria in the stomachs of wood-eating termites to find the enzymes that break down cellulose.

CASE STUDY

Pig Manure for Vehicles

The methane made when bacteria feed on manure may be processed into biodiesel rather than burned. Methane is trickier to store and transport than biodiesel, and cannot be easily used in vehicles. In the U.S., meat-processing plants keep millions of pigs that produce enormous lakes of liquid manure, or slurry. The slurry represents a pollution hazard if it washes into rivers. Some scientists working for Smithfield Foods in Utah view the slurry as fuel for vehicles. They have developed a process that changes the slurry into methane and then converts the methane into a type of alcohol called methanol, which is then combined with fats to make biodiesel. The fats are obtained from waste oil from meat processing or from soybeans. The scientists believe this process could get rid of Smithfield's slurry problem and produce 40,000 gallons (150,000 liters) of biodiesel each day.

The Future for Biomass Power

Biomass should have a bright future in the coming decades. It is a versatile energy resource that can be used in many settings, from power plants to mopeds, in solid, liquid, or gas form. At its best, biomass is renewable, has a low impact on global warming, and can be as efficient or cheap as fossil fuel power. At its worst, biomass creates atmospheric and environmental problems and food shortages.

Growth in Biomass

Scientists estimate that enough biomass grows each year to supply around a sixth of the world's fuel and electricity needs. They predict that the big growth areas will be production of bioethanol from cellulose in plant waste and biodiesel from algae. These could replace around 10 percent of the fossil fuel equivalents by 2030. Whether or not this happens will depend on government investment in biomass research and technology, and the impacts of energy crops such as corn and oil palm on global habitats and people. The great unknown for biomass is global warming—changing weather could damage biomass plantations, but warmer air temperatures may make biomass plants grow faster.

Richard Branson, owner of Virgin Atlantic, demonstrated the potential of biofuels for air travel in 2008 by fueling a flight partly with coconut oil.

Changing Energy Use

Some scientists believe biomass is not the whole answer to the fuel crisis. However, they believe that it could provide an alternative to fossil fuels until such time as renewables, such as solar power or **hydrogen cells,** are more widespread. However, before the solar and hydrogen technologies are ready for general use, scientists argue that saving energy by using less is more important in reducing global warming than using more biomass. For example, in 2009, global biomass produced just over one percent of electricity, yet leaving electrical machines such as TVs on standby wasted over four times as much!

Cycling is a growing transportation solution that uses no fuel and creates no emissions. It also keeps riders fit.

CASE STUDY   Closing the Loop

In 2009, landfill gas from the Altamont site in California was first used for fuel in waste-recovery trucks that deliver waste to the site. The gas is cooled and condensed into liquid gas in the largest landfill-to-liquid-gas factory in the world. Using waste to create biofuel that is used to deliver more waste is one example of a closed loop system. Although burning the gas releases carbon dioxide, removing the landfill gas prevents the far more harmful greenhouse gas methane from trapping heat in the atmosphere.

Biomass Activity

What you need:
- Small bag/can of unsalted, shelled peanuts
- Cork and needle
- Large metal juice or coffee can
- Small metal can (such as a soup can) with paper label removed
- Can opener
- Hammer and large nail
- Metal BBQ skewer
- Thermometer
- Lighter
- Paper and pencil
- An adult helper

Peanut Fuel!

Peanut oil was used as biodiesel in one of the first demonstration diesel engines at the turn of the twentieth century. Demonstrate the energy in a single peanut by using it as fuel to heat up water.

1 Ask an adult to carefully push the eye of the needle into the smaller end of the cork and the point into a peanut. If it breaks, use another peanut.

2 Ask an adult to punch holes with a hammer and nail around the bottom of the large can (letting in air will help the peanut burn) and also two exactly opposite each other at the top of the small can.

3 Remove the ends of the large juice can and one end of the small one with the can opener. BE CAREFUL—the cut edges are sharp!

4 Place the cork and peanut on a surface that will not burn, such as a tile. Light the peanut with the lighter with an adult's help. Half fill the small can with water and record its temperature.

5 Place the big can over the burning nut, then slide the BBQ skewer through the holes of the small can and sit that on the big can.

6 Allow the nut to burn for several minutes or until it goes out. Then stir the water with the thermometer and record the temperature again.

7 Now repeat the demonstration with different types of nuts, and different amounts of water. How did your results vary?

Cooker with peanut power

- small can
- skewer
- large can
- peanut
- cork
- air holes

Biomass Topics and Glossary

History
- Look at the timelines of energy at http://tonto.eia.doe.gov/kids/energy.cfm?page=4. Create your own for biomass using these resources.

Geography
- Find out about sustainable agriculture and examples of sustainable biomass production.

Design and Technology
- Design a promotional leaflet from an oil company describing the benefits of biofuels to drivers and the planet—include some quotations about biofuels you find in newspapers or on the Internet.

English
- Can you imagine gas stations with algae tanks to make biodiesel? Write a short story about a traveler in the future when biomass power is the main energy source.

Science
- Palm oil is one of the world's major crops. Research the properties that make palm oil so widely used. Are there any alternatives to palm oil?

Glossary

bacteria tiny, simple living things.

biodiesel fuel made from organic raw materials, not fossil fuel oil, that can be used in diesel engines.

biodigester tank in which bacteria decompose organic matter.

biodiversity measure of the range of types of living thing in an area.

bioethanol (fuel ethanol) alcohol from fermentation of biomass used as biofuel for vehicles.

biofuel renewable fuels made from biomass.

climate normal pattern of weather over a long period of time.

cofire to burn two fuels at the same time.

combined heat and power (CHP) generating and using both electricity and heat from a power station.

coppice to harvest stems from trees that grow more stems.

decompose naturally break down, or rot, into chemicals.

deforestation cutting down or burning natural forest or woodland.

enzyme substance produced by living things that speeds up a chemical reaction.

food aid food given to those in need, usually by one country to another.

fossil fuel fuel formed over millions of years underground from the remains of living things.

fuelwood wood used as fuel for burning.

global warming increase in the average temperature of the atmosphere and oceans.

greenhouse gas gas such as carbon dioxide that stores heat in the atmosphere.

habitat place where a particular type of living thing is normally found.

hydroelectric power using moving fresh water in rivers or from reservoirs to generate electricity.

hydrogen cell device turning hydrogen and oxygen into water and generating electricity.

landfill gas gas used as fuel that forms when landfill waste decomposes.

nonrenewable energy resource such as coal that is running out because it is not replaced when used.

nutrient substance needed to keep a living thing alive, healthy, and able to grow.

organic produced by living things.

peat soil containing partly rotted plants.

photosynthesis process by which green plants make food in leaves using energy from sunlight.

plantation area of land where a single crop such as biomass is grown.

renewable energy resource that is replaced naturally and can be used without running out.

Further Information, Web Sites, and Index

Books

Energy and the Environment: Biofuels
by John Tabak
(Facts on File, 2009)

Energy Now and In the Future:
  Biomass Power
by Neil Morris
(Smart Apple Media, 2009)

The World of Energy: Understanding
  Geothermal Energy and Bioenergy
by Fiona Reynoldson
(Gareth Stevens Publishing, 2010)

Web Sites

Due to the changing nature of Internet links, PowerKids Press has developed an online list of Web sites related to the subject of this book. This site is updated regularly. Please use this link to access this list:
http://www.powerkidslinks.com/lder/biomass/

Index